EXTREME
Pumpkin Carving

Written by Vic Hood
Photography by Jack A. Williams

Fox Chapel
PUBLISHING

© 2004 by Vic Hood and Fox Chapel Publishing Company, Inc., East Petersburg, PA.

Extreme Pumpkin Carving is an original work, first published in 2004 by Fox Chapel Publishing Company, Inc. The patterns contained herein are copyrighted by the artists named. Readers may make copies of these patterns for personal use. The patterns themselves, however, are not to be duplicated for resale or distribution under any circumstances. Any such copying is a violation of copyright law.

ISBN 978-1-56523-213-6

Library of Congress Cataloging-in-Publication Data

Hood, Vic.
    Extreme pumpkin carving / written by Vic Hood ; photography by Jack A. Williams.
       p. cm.
    ISBN 1-56523-213-5 (pbk. : alk. paper)
    1. Halloween decorations. 2. Jack-o-lanterns. I. Title.
    TT900.H32H66 2004
    745.594'1646—dc22
                                2004040369

To learn more about the other great books from Fox Chapel Publishing, or to find a retailer near you, call toll-free 800-457-9112 or visit us at *www.FoxChapelPublishing.com*.

Note to Authors: We are always looking for talented authors to write new books. Please send a brief letter describing your idea to Acquisition Editor, 1970 Broad Street, East Petersburg, PA 17520.

Printed in the United States of America
Fourth printing

ACKNOWLEDGMENTS

We authors would like to extend appreciation to all of the pumpkin carvers who allowed us to showcase their award-winning pumpkins in the pattern section of this book. All of these pumpkins were carved during The Great Pumpkin Carving Competition (2002 and 2003) at Dollywood in Pigeon Forge, Tennessee.

Vic wishes to thank Allen and Cindy Gentry of the Gentry Pumpkin Harvest Farm in Franklin, Tennessee, for allowing the authors to use their facility for background and for providing pumpkins to carve.

Jack wishes to thank Dollywood's Director of Special Events, Dave Anderson, for giving his support in 1996 to hold the first Great Pumpkin Carving Competition at the Dollywood Woodcarving Showcase, which gave birth to the style of pumpkin carving illustrated in this book.

Together, we wish to thank Dollywood's Special Events Manager, Jane Groff, for always being available to assist in this event.

We would like to recognize Carole Williams for her significant contribution in photographic preparation, and Dona Antonelli for drawing the patterns.

ABOUT THE AUTHORS

 **Vic Hood** is the president of a unique building corporation, Leatherwood, Inc., which specializes in historic restoration. As a restorationist, Vic has been responsible for the restoration of several presidential houses, national landmarks, national monuments and house museums. He started carving in 1991, concentrating on carving full-size human busts for which he has won 83 awards, including several Best of Show awards. His most treasured honor was to be selected to create a Christmas ornament for the White House in 2001. Vic is one of the founders of the Leipers Fork Carving Club in Leipers Fork, Tennessee.

Vic studied carving under John Burke and Larry Rogers for several years before becoming a carving instructor himself. He currently teaches classes on carving the human bust at several major workshops around the country and at individual club workshops. Due to Vic's experience in competitive pumpkin carving, he was invited to be the featured pumpkin carver at the 2003 Gentry Farms Pumpkin Festival.

Vic, along with Jack Williams, co-authored *Carving Found Wood*, published by Fox Chapel Publishing Co., Inc.

 **Jack A. Williams** is a retired commercial photographer living in Sun City West, Arizona with his wife, Carole. Photography was once a hobby for Jack until he discovered he could make a living doing what he enjoyed. He then needed a new hobby, so in 1973 he started woodcarving. His artistic talents have been demonstrated with a Third Best of Show in the first National Caricature Carving Competition held at Silver Dollar City in Branson, Missouri; a Best of Show at the Ward Wildfowl Carving Competition in Ocean City, Maryland; People's and Carver's Choice and Best of Wood Sculpture at Dollywood in Pigeon Forge, Tennessee; and Best of Division at the International Woodcarvers Congress in Davenport, Iowa. He also won first place in the Flex-Cut Tool Internet Carving Competition in 2001.

Jack coordinated the Dollywood Woodcarving Showcase for fifteen years and the National Caricature Carving Competition for four years. In 2003, Jack was elected to become a member of the Caricature Carvers of America and is one of the founders of the Tennessee Carvers Guild. Jack now spends a great deal of time photographing carvings at shows and for friends, and his photography appears frequently in many magazines on woodcarving and other subjects.

Jack is a co-author of *Extreme Pumpkin Carving* and *Carving Found Wood* with Vic Hood, *The Illustrated Guide to Carving Tree Bark* with Rick Jensen, and *Carving Cypress Knees* with Carole Jean Boyd, all published by Fox Chapel Publishing Company, Inc.

CONTENTS

INTRODUCTION

It is difficult for anyone to think of a fruit or vegetable that can stir the imagination of both children and adults alike more than a pumpkin. From the *Legend of Sleepy Hollow* to Cinderella's coach, the pumpkin has been represented in our culture as a magical fruit. This perception had its beginnings in pumpkin carving for Halloween, a holiday celebrated for centuries by early Celts, witches and some religious groups as the most magical night of the year. Today the religious significance has passed for most people, but Halloween still remains a magical night with pumpkins as an integral part of this celebration.

Pumpkin carving is becoming more popular every year. Through time pumpkin carving has evolved from simple, pierced jack-o'-lanterns to elaborate portraitures and now to surface carving. The style of carving presented in this book is a relief-carving technique, a presentation that has been borrowed from stone and woodcarving. Relief carving relies on perspective and shadows to develop the image and provides more opportunity for creative options. With this technique you will be able to add form to your pumpkin carving by creating actual cheeks, lips, eyebrows and more, instead of just cutting out solid shapes.

GETTING STARTED

Extreme pumpkin carving applies relief-carving techniques, commonly found in woodworking and stonework, to pumpkins. Starting with solid pumpkins (no hollowing is necessary!), extreme pumpkin carvers use woodcarving gouges and knives to create fantastic faces and scenes in the flesh of the pumpkins.

A BRIEF HISTORY OF HALLOWEEN

Most people think of Halloween as a night to dress up in ghostly or funny costumes, to have parties, or to go "trick-or-treating" and never consider why or how such a holiday evolved from a serious annual rite in ancient times. What is actually being celebrated is two customs that have been combined into one.

I personally like to use tall, elongated pumpkins for extreme pumpkin carvings; however, any size pumpkin with thick flesh will work just fine.

RIGHT: Make sure the pumpkin you choose is ripe. Ripeness is indicated by uniform color.

OPPOSITE PAGE
TOP: Many varieties of field pumpkins grow the thick flesh that is key to creating an extreme pumpkin carving. Gold Rush, Half Moon and Pankow's Field are several of my favorite varieties.

BOTTOM: Extreme pumpkin carving is a great activity for Halloween aficionados; however, it is not recommended for small children who have no experience controlling sharp carving tools.

The first tradition is the observance of a Catholic religious day set aside to honor saints. Referred to as "All Hallows Day" or "All Saints Day," this holy day is held on November 1st. The night before is known as "All Hallows Eve," from which the name Halloween evolved.

The second celebration is from Northern France and the British Isles where the Celtic people celebrated the end of the Celtic year known as Samhain (pronounced sow-en) or "Summer's End." This festival was a time set aside to honor the dead. The Celts believed that the realm of the dead, or the spirit world, and the physical world were closest together during Samhain.

The traditional celebration of Samhain included carving jack-o'-lanterns from gourds and turnips, then lighting them with coals or candles to show the way for deceased loved ones. At the same time, these lanterns were believed to ward off evil spirits. Another version of this celebration indicates that disembodied spirits of those that died during

state. To be released, the devil agreed to leave Jack's soul alone for ten years.

After ten years had passed, the devil appeared to Jack as he was walking down a country road. The silver-tongued Jack managed to talk the devil into climbing an apple tree before claiming his soul. While the devil was in the tree, Jack pulled out his knife and carved a cross in the base of the tree, thus trapping the devil again. Again he struck a bargain with the devil, this time extracting a promise that the devil would never take his soul.

When Jack finally died, he went to Heaven but was not allowed in because of his drinking and dastardly ways. With no place to go, he went to Hell. The devil, remembering Jack's trickery, refused him entrance. Jack then convinced the devil that the way back was so dark and windy that he needed a light to find his way. To get rid of Jack, the devil gave him an ember from Hell. Jack placed the ember in a turnip he was eating to shield the flame from the wind and began to wander back in the darkness, forever doomed.

SELECTING A PUMPKIN

First, have an idea of what you want to carve and then select the shape that will best accommodate the design. Some designs work better on small, rounded pumpkins; other designs work well on larger, elongated ones. Most of my pumpkin carvings are done on tall, narrow pumpkins because that shape makes it easier for me to carve a well-tapered face that is not too flat.

Second, look for a pumpkin variety that has thick flesh. The more depth in the flesh of the pumpkin, the better the opportunity to fully

the year intermingled with the living on that night. They attempted to possess the living in hopes of being allowed to have an afterlife. In an effort to frighten away the spirits, people would leave their houses unlit and cold, dress up in ghoulish costumes, and parade around town being as destructive as possible. This tradition set the stage for today's children's refrain "trick or treat." When the Europeans arrived in the New World, they discovered a new fruit that was larger than a turnip and easier to carve: the pumpkin. The pumpkin

has been the symbol of Halloween ever since.

The story of the name jack-o'-lantern has a history of its own. It derives from a folk tale about a disreputable drunkard by the name of Jack who, upon learning that the devil had come for his soul, tricked the devil into buying him one last drink. Having no money, Jack convinced the devil to transform himself into coins so that Jack could buy his last drink. Instead of buying the drink, Jack placed the coins in his pocket along with a silver cross, thus preventing the devil from returning to his common develop the carved features. One way to ascertain if the pumpkin has thick flesh is to determine its relative weight. Heavier pumpkins tend to have thick flesh while lighter pumpkins of the same size will have thinner flesh. Some suggested varieties that have thick flesh include Gold Rush, Half Moon and Pankow's Field.

Third, select a pumpkin that is ripe. Ripeness is indicated by uniform color. Be sure there are no bruises, cuts or nicks, because these defects will shorten the life of your carving.

PRESERVING PUMPKINS

Pumpkin carvings will not last long. I have tried pickling them, treating them with fungicide, covering them in lemon juice, smothering them with petroleum jelly, and putting a finish on them. My best results have come from spraying the cut surface with a polyacrylic finish. This will prevent the pumpkin from drying out so fast and will extend the life of the carving. When spraying a carving with finish, be sure to do it outside or in a well-ventilated area. Dry the surface of the pumpkin with a cloth or paper towels before applying the finish.

There are other things that can be done to extend the life of a pumpkin. Pumpkins begin to shrivel because of the loss of water. By soaking your carved pumpkin in water overnight, you can extend its life. You can also make your pumpkin carving last longer by keeping it out of the sun in a cool, dry location. When you are not displaying your pumpkin, place it in a refrigerator to slow down the decomposition. You may also want to try Pumpkin Preserver, which is a low cost, environmentally friendly product that slows down the deterioration of pumpkins by deterring mold, rot and bugs.

To extend the life of your carving indefinitely, use an artificial pumpkin. Artificial pumpkins are made from foam that can be carved.

• PUMPKIN FACTS •

- Pumpkin seeds can be roasted as a snack.
- Pumpkins contain potassium and Vitamin A.
- Pumpkins are used for feed for animals.
- Pumpkin flowers are edible.
- Pumpkins are members of the vine crops family called *cucurbits*, which also includes melons, gourds, cucumbers and gherkins.
- Pumpkins originated in Central America.
- In early colonial times, pumpkins were used as an ingredient for the crusts of pies, not for the filling.
- Pumpkins were once recommended for removing freckles and curing snakebites.
- Pumpkins range in size from less than a pound to over 1,000 pounds.

- The name pumpkin originated from *pepon*, the Greek word for large melon.
- The Connecticut Field variety is the traditional American pumpkin.
- Pumpkins are 90 percent water.
- Pumpkins are fruit.
- Eighty percent of the pumpkin supply in the United States is available in October.
- In colonial times, Native Americans roasted long strips of pumpkin on an open fire.
- Colonists sliced off pumpkin tips, removed seeds and filled the insides with milk, spices and honey. This was baked in hot ashes and is the origin of pumpkin pie.

- Native Americans flattened strips of pumpkins, dried them and made mats.
- Native Americans called pumpkins "isqoutm squash".
- Native Americans used pumpkin seeds for food and medicine.
- Pumpkins are low in calories, fat and sodium and high in fiber.
- They are a good source of Vitamins A and B, potassium, protein and iron.
- Originally turnips were used for jack-o'-lanterns.
- The practice of carving fruits and vegetables came from Celtic traditions.
- Pumpkins are a variety of squash.

PART TWO

EXTREME PUMPKIN CARVING

In this chapter, two approaches are used to carve pumpkins in this unique relief-carved style. In the first step-by-step demonstration, only readily available knives are used. This process was photographed to demonstrate that it does not take expensive—and sometimes difficult-to-handle—tools to create an interesting pumpkin carving. Using this method, you will not have to buy anything but a pumpkin to get started.

The second step-by-step presentation was completed using woodcarving tools. Creating a relief-carved pumpkin is easier and faster with woodcarving tools, and those tools are the inspiration behind the development of this technique. Most people who work with woodcarving tools will find the second approach more familiar.

In both step-by-step approaches, the process is the same; the only difference is in the use and the deployment of various tools.

USING READILY AVAILABLE KNIVES TO RELIEF-CARVE A PUMPKIN

PART TWO

• TOOLS •

- Permanent fine-line marker
- Permanent heavy-line felt-tip marker
- Single blade knife or pocket knife
- Butcher knife
- Old toothbrush
- Finish nail and/or pounce wheel
- Masking tape

For most of my pumpkin carvings, I select a tall, elongated pumpkin because it is easier to develop the pitch of the face in the horizontal plane. In other words, the extra height of a taller pumpkin allows you to carve a larger nose and to create darker shadows and stronger features, thereby creating a more interesting carving.

To start a pumpkin carving, sketch your idea on paper first. To transfer your idea to the pumpkin, start with a centerline to ensure symmetry. Here a permanent fine-line marker is used. A permanent marker won't smear and the fine line will enable you to adjust the proportions.

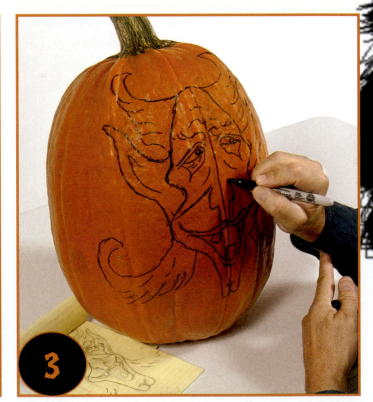

After you have made your final decisions on layout and proportion, use a larger felt-tip permanent marker to sketch the final drawing. Redraw the centerline. If you are hesitant about your drawing skills, try attaching a drawing to the pumpkin and using carbon paper or a pounce wheel to transfer the image.

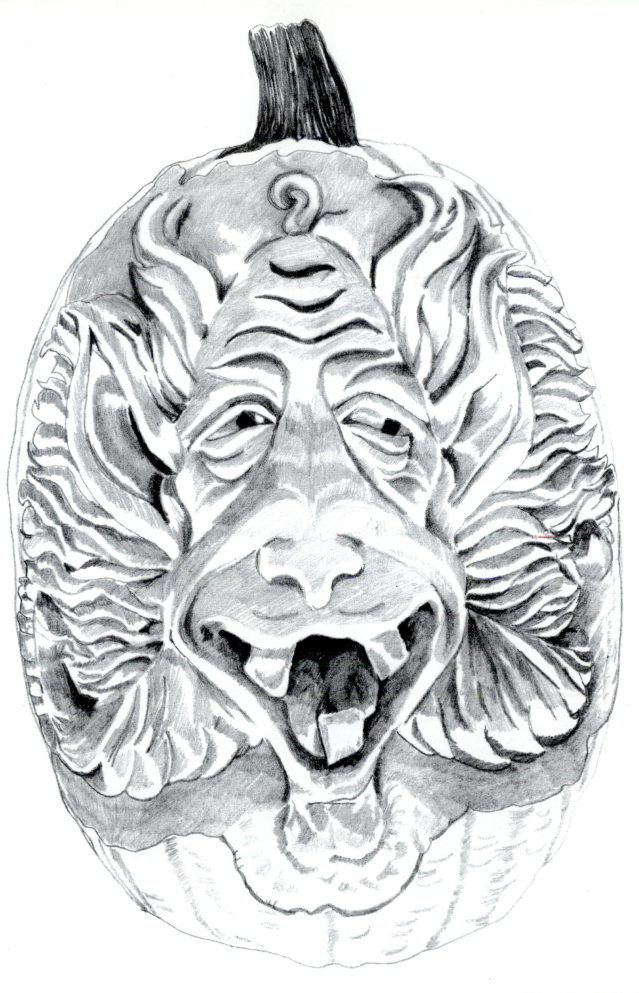

4

5

If you place the pattern too low, it is difficult to see; if it is too high the carving looks awkward. Here the drawing is complete and has a well-balanced presentation both horizontally and vertically. Try to design a carving that is large enough to cover one side of the pumpkin but small enough to allow the orange skin to frame the carving. Framing will give the carving added definition and depth.

Start by outlining the face. This will keep the design intact and allow you to start creating the depth that will be necessary to properly develop features. Note that, unlike traditional jack-o'-lanterns, relief-carved pumpkins are not hollowed out.

6

7

In this design it is important to keep the outline cut perpendicular to the surface to maintain the integrity of the design. In the initial layout most people do not make this cut deep enough for fear they will cut through the pumpkin. Close attention to the meat will prevent you from cutting too deep. As the cut gets near the interior, the meat of the pumpkin will get soft and mushy. Here I have cut an inch and a half deep.

After outlining the perimeter of the face, I start outlining the most prominent feature: the nose. I want the nose to be the highest point of the carving and the rest of the facial features to be recessed behind the nose.

To maintain the design and to assist in getting depth, the "laugh line" is cut in with a shallow cut. This will be cut deeper later on in the carving.

It is important to "pull the nose out of the face" by removing material from around it while maintaining the original design.

Trim the area above the laugh line back to give the nose depth and to start creating a cheek. The right side has already been removed. Note how the cheek is starting to develop. With this cut, the eye design and placement remain intact.

From the center of the nose, make a smooth transition cut to the outside depth of the outline cut. This will pull the nose forward and help round the face.

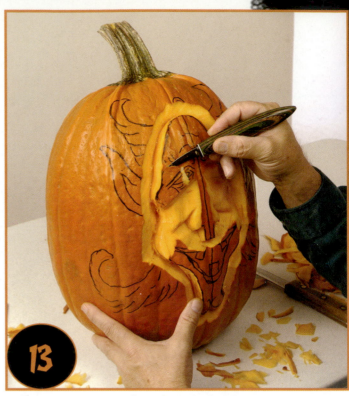

Be sure to take the cut all the way to the outline of the face. This will help to give the illusion of depth.

Make a stop cut to start forming the ball of the eye.

Remove material to the stop cut in a round motion to mimic the roundness of the eye.

On the outside edge of the face at the eye socket, make an angle cut to start the rounding process of the eye from side to side.

16

Make a stop cut on the bottom of the eye socket and remove the material in a circular motion to create a roundness to the eye.

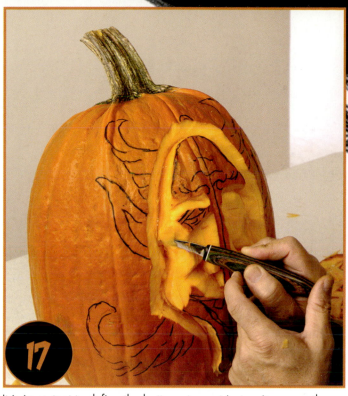

17

It is important to define the bottom stop cut just as it was on the top of the eye socket.

18

The last stop cut is made on the interior of the eye socket. It is cut in a diagonal direction away from the center of the nose.

19

With a rounding motion, remove the material to the stop cut.

20

To complete the eye socket, all of the stop cuts should be defined by this point in the process.

21

After the perimeter of the eye socket is defined, round the eyeball into the socket so that it is rounded both horizontally and vertically.

22

Narrow the bridge of the nose, defining the interior edge of the eye at the same time.

23

Begin to remove the edge area of the face, rounding it into the outline of the face. At the same time, push the forehead back to give dimension to the face and the surrounding features.

PART TWO

24

Just as with the face, start to outline the features surrounding the carving.

25

Be sure to make your outline stop cuts perpendicular to the surface and deep.

26

Remove the material down to the stop cut in an angled, but steep, cut. This will help later on to frame the carving.

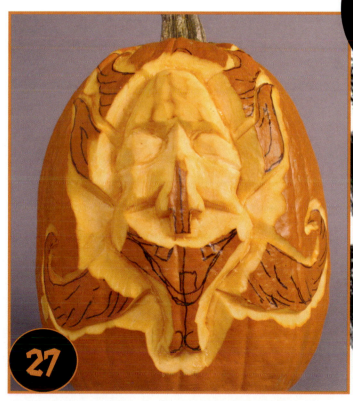

27

This is what the pumpkin carving should look like at this stage. The face is rounded, and the forms of all of the features are defined, except the mouth. Note the depth and definition of the eyes as well as the depth around the base of the nose.

28

Using the outline of the features as a stop cut, bring the form out by cutting in at an angle. This cut will differ from the earlier cuts because this cut will form the basis of the hair.

29

After the feature has been defined, make an angle cut to taper the feature into the face. This will give dimension to the face and leave material to develop detail on the hair and ears.

30

As the features are defined, watch for the opportunity to increase the dimensions of the features by further defining and rounding the carving.

31

It is now possible to remove more material from the forehead, allowing you to taper the nose to the brow line. In the process, all of the exterior skin can be removed from the nose.

32

In order to get a proper setting for the eyes, the bottom of the eye socket is pushed back.

33

At this juncture, all of the exterior skin can be removed because you can see where all of the features are outlined.

34

Now that the form of the carving is established, the detail work can begin. Starting with the side of the nose, make an angle cut to form the nostril.

35

To form the underside of the nostril, make an angle cut toward the center of the nose. Removing these horizontal lines will give the nose more interest.

PART TWO

A transition cut from the laugh line to the nostril will break the sharp edge that was created when outlining the face.

Round the nostril. Note the finished rounding on the left side.

PART TWO

To detail the eye, start by softening the brow line and making a smooth transition into the eyelid.

Make the top of the eye by slicing a stop cut from the top of the eye to the tear duct.

40

Make a second stop cut from the top of the eye to the outside edge of the eye socket.

41

Remove the material under the eye. This will form the upper eyelid.

42

To form the lower lid, make a stop cut from the outside corner to the interior tear duct.

43

Remove the material between the two eyelids, taking care to maintain the round eyeball structure. I typically remove a little more in the corners to help round the eyes.

44

At this point, the eye is roughed in. It is important to maintain the roundness and proper shape so that the detail appears anatomically correct.

45

Remove a small triangle on the outside of the eye to create a shadow. This will give the eye more dimension and a sense of roundness.

PART TWO

46

Remove a similar cut from the tear duct on the interior of the eye. This shadow cut will make the eye round.

47

Join the shadow lines at the bottom to form a bag under the eye.

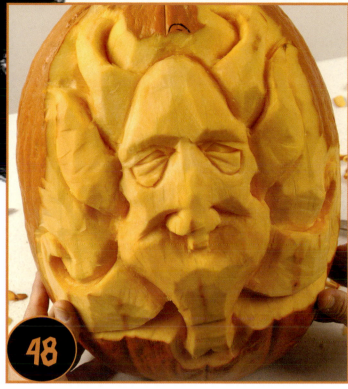

Notice how much more dimension the shadow lines give the eyes.

To increase the intensity of the shadows, make a deep shadow cut under the eyelids. Notice how much more visible the eyelid on the right is after the shadow cut.

Make a defining cut at the bridge of the nose, which will imply the presence of eyebrows.

It is time to form the mouth by making an incision into the area below the nose. This is not a straight cut but two slow arches that meet in the center below the nose.

Remove the interior of the mouth using a sharp angle cut. This will allow the formation of the lips on the exterior and create the steep angle on the interior, which will facilitate the creation of the teeth.

It is important to develop as much interior shadow as possible to define the lips.

Now that the interior of the mouth is defined, carve the teeth by making stop cuts and removing the interior.

Removing material around the teeth will bring out the overall shape of the teeth. Be sure to get a deep shadow in the corner of the mouth.

Cut the lower tooth at an angle to provide added shadow and to show the tooth much better.

Taking out the area in the corner of the mouth and behind the tooth will provide shadow, which will help with the illusion of roundness.

Remove the material in the center of the mouth in order to cut in the tongue.

Remove the front of the teeth to push them back into the mouth and to provide a deep shadow under the lip.

I decided to remove material from around the chin area to make a more dramatic presentation. Giving a feature more depth and shadow makes the feature stand out. Removing material at a slight angle under the chin adds to the effect.

Another way to develop dimension is to capture shadows in lines and wrinkles. The addition of lines and wrinkles to this carving gives the piece more character.

Take a look at your progress to this point. You may discover that you need to make some alterations to the original pattern to get the "look" you want. I have decided to increase the amount of shadow by connecting the cheek cut to the cut on the bridge of the nose. As you become more comfortable carving pumpkins in relief these decisions to deviate from the original pattern will become more obvious.

When making wrinkles and lines, the outer edges need to have soft rolls. These soft rolls will create highlights and prevent the lines from becoming too static and looking like knife cuts rather than forms.

PART TWO

64

Here I am better defining the exterior of the mouth by putting in some small wrinkle lines.

65

After standing back and looking at the development of the features, I have decided to increase the shadow value of the laugh line by putting a hard line in the bottom of the feature.

66

While assessing the laugh line, I determined that the nose needs more shaping and thinning. Here I am adding more shadow to the nostril and rounding it more.

67

I have also determined that the transition area between the nose and the cheek is too heavy and that the nose is too wide. Here I am simply trimming down this area until it looks gaunt (a look I was initially hoping to create).

68

I also decided to undercut the nose so that it would stand out.

69

At this point, review the pumpkin again. I am satisfied that this face is nicely laid out and well defined; however, I intend to put more detail in once I have defined the ears and hair with shadow and definition.

PART TWO

70

The shadowing and feature definition is done in much the same way as the features of the face. Start by cutting a stop cut in the ear.

71

Remove material at an angle inside the ear. This is important because the slant not only produces shadow, but it also gives the ear a form that will make an appropriate presentation.

72

Here you can see the effectiveness of the slant. Notice the shadow that brings the form of the ears out.

73

To create the maximum amount of interest and appeal in a carving, you need a lot of movement. The hair is one area where movement can be accomplished with relative ease. In creating the hairlines, be sure to make the strands wave.

74

First cut the hair into groups of strands. After the movement of the hair is established, break up a few of the strands so they do not run continuously. By breaking up the strands, you do not give the same shadow value to every part of the hair. This also helps to create more movement.

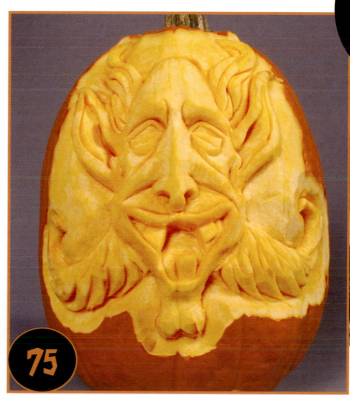

75

Now all of the features have been laid out and defined. Note how the hair patches coming out of the cheeks are broken up on the ends, defining each hair strand.

76

Begin to make the final cuts on the face. Starting with wrinkles, a wedge is cut out to separate the highlight areas and to create a deep shadow.

77

Once the highlight areas are separated and the deep shadow is established, soften the edges of the cuts so they roll into the crevice.

78

To make the eyes more dramatic, make a shadow cut to define the underlying eye socket. This cut also creates an eyebrow.

79

This photo illustrates how much more dramatic the eyes are when the eye sockets are broken up.

PART TWO

Cut in the pupil of the eye by going all the way through the meat of the pumpkin.

One simple way to add to the movement of a carving is to have the subject looking at something. Cutting the pupil through the pumpkin adds life to the pumpkin; the movement in his eyes reinforces it.

Add dark lines to the bags under the eyes to give them more emphasis.

Better define the cheek line and add a shadow by extending the cut from the bridge of the nose to the outside of the cheek.

Add hair all around the carving. Use the same method as described in Step 74. To distinguish this hair from the larger tuffs carved earlier, make the strands in shorter strokes with a lot of movement. I chose to run the hair into the undisturbed skin of the pumpkin to aid in contrast and movement.

To get the maximum amount of shadow in the mouth, cut a hole through the meat of the pumpkin in the same way that you cut the eyes. Cut in the center groove for the tongue to finish the carving.

Dry the surface of the pumpkin with a cloth or paper towels, then spray the pumpkin with a polyacrylic finish to extend its life.

87

This is the finished carving. A typical pumpkin carving of this size
takes between one-and-a-half and two hours.

USING WOODCARVING TOOLS TO RELIEF-CARVE A PUMPKIN

• TOOLS •

- Permanent fine-line marker
- Permanent heavy-line felt-tip marker
- Carving knife
- #41 v-tool
- #16, 6 mm v-tool
- #3, 7 mm flat gouge
- #5, 25 mm gouge
- #6, 12 mm gouge
- #7, 25 mm gouge
- #11, 3 mm gouge
- #11, 10 mm gouge
- #11, 12 mm gouge
- Finish nail and/or pounce wheel
- Masking tape

In this demonstration I will be using carving tools to relief-carve the pumpkin. Because I am more familiar with these implements, it is an easier and faster process. To complete a carving of this size will take approximately an hour.

2

The technique for using carving tools is different than using a knife, but the process is about the same. Begin by outlining the outside of the face. Use a v-tool to preserve the design as long as possible.

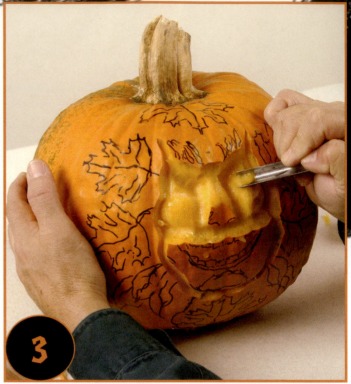

3

Develop the structure for the nose by pushing back the rest of the face and recessing the eye sockets. Use a #5, 25 mm gouge to clear away the flat area. Use a #11, 12 mm to cut the grooves under and beside the nose and to recess the eye socket.

4

Develop the round end of the nose with a #6, 12 mm. Create a nice, round nose tip by starting at the tip and rolling the gouge under the nose.

5

Use the same #6, 12 mm to put curvature in the base of the nostril.

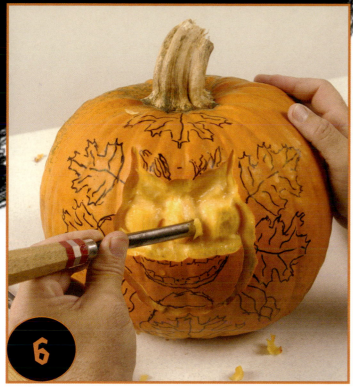

6

Use the #6, 12 mm to form the side and top of the nostril. This tool has enough curvature to form the nostril in one cut. It is important to pay attention to the angle of the cut: Don't make it perpendicular to the face.

7

To form the puffy cheeks, use a #7, 25 mm in a rounding motion.

8

Lay in the eyes by using a knife incision as a stop cut for the top and bottom eyelids.

9

Using a #7, 25 mm, remove material from above the eye to allow for softening of the eye socket.

10

Cut in the bags under the eyes with a #11, 3 mm. The left side is finished.

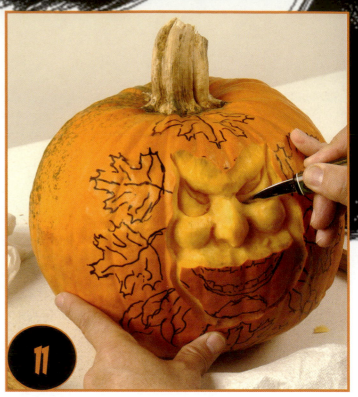

11

With a knife, create a dark shadow line in the #11 cut that created the bags under the eyes.

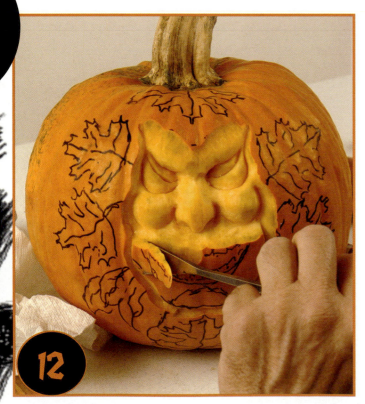

12

Round the mouth with the #7, 25 mm in preparation for carving the lips. It is very important to develop proper form prior to cutting the detail.

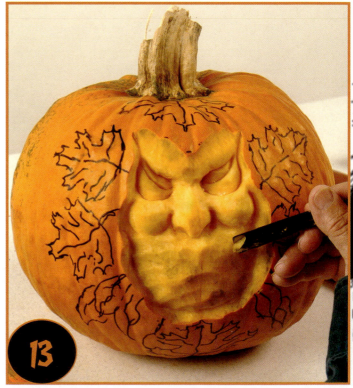

13

Cut a bow-shaped lip area with a #11, 10 mm. The #11 is used to provide a soft development of the upper lip. This will allow the upper lip to be easily rolled into the teeth.

Using a v-tool, follow the center of the #11 cut. With this cut you can see the beginning of the upper lip.

Form the lower lip by cutting the outline of the inside of the mouth, making sure to leave enough room for large teeth.

Place a shadow line under the upper lip with a knife. This cut is made as preparation for carving the teeth.

Remove the corners of the interior of the mouth to make the mouth more parabolic and to create a shadow in the corner of the mouth. The interior shadow provides the viewer's eye with a vanishing point to make the dentition look as if it has depth.

18

Push the face back and extend the cheekbone to pull the face out of the pumpkin more and to allow for the development of facial features.

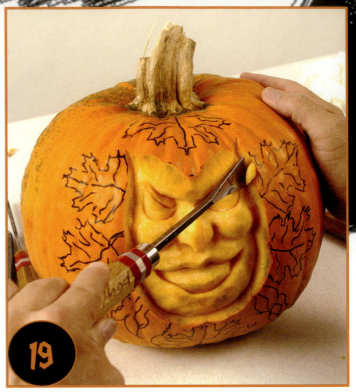

19

Narrowing the area above the eye gives movement to the face and at the same time, creates a shadow that will help to define the face. I am using a #7, 25 mm to make this cut because the curvature of this tool provides just enough movement without overdoing it.

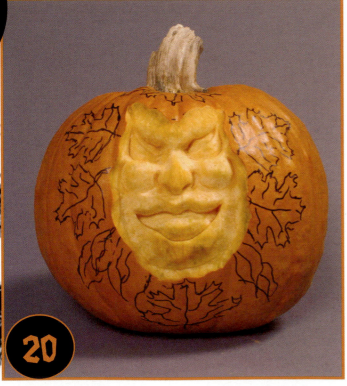

20

At this point, all of the features of the face are roughed in and ready for detail work. Notice how all of the forms of the face are prepared in a soft presentation with shadow separations.

21

Use a v-tool to outline the leaves that surround the face. The leaves will be left with the exterior skin to provide some design contrast to the face.

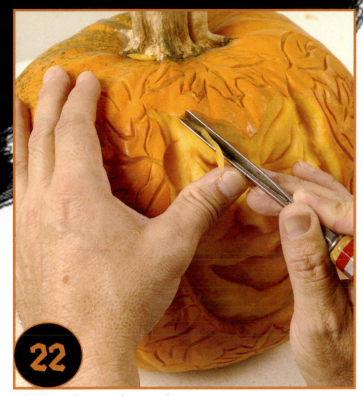

Add the eyebrow with a v-tool.

Lay in the bags under the eyes with a small v-tool. The eyes will be finished with a knife cut in the final detailing.

Although the v-tool made a good form cut, it did not provide a deep enough shadow to bring out the lines in the face; therefore, all of the cuts made with the v-tool need to be followed with a knife.

Cut the pupils through the meat of the pumpkin to get the maximum amount of shadow value. Shift them to one side for movement.

26

Continue to add detail around the mouth by putting in shadow lines below the cheeks and around the mouth.

27

Cut the center groove between the mouth and the nose using a #11, 3 mm.

28

Form the bottom lip by cutting a groove under the lip with a #11, 10 mm.

29

With a #16, 6 mm v-tool, outline the centerline of the teeth.

Better define the centerline by using a knife cut to create a deep shadow.

Cut in the teeth using a knife.

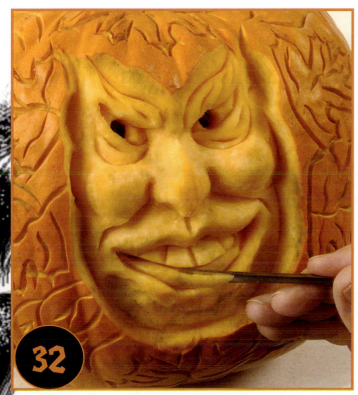

Use a #3, 7 mm to recess the lower row of teeth. This cut will give a good shadow line that will make both sets of teeth show up better.

Sharpen the separation of the teeth and lips with a knife.

34

Cut a deep shadow to increase the vanishing point of the dental arch.

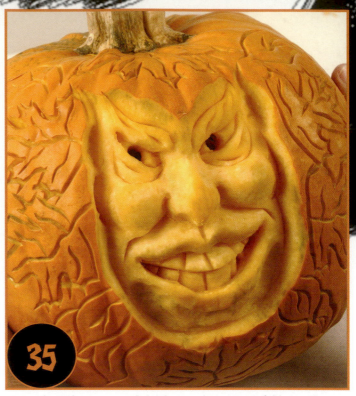

35

Notice how the increased shadow in the corner of the mouth increased the depth and dimension of the dental arch.

36

Using a knife, make a deep shadow cut under the nostrils.

37

To clean up the edge of the carving around the face and to bring the features forward, make an angular cut around the face.

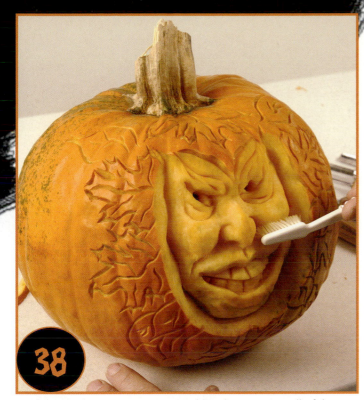

38

To clean up the carving, use a toothbrush to get into all of the crevices.

39

Using a polyacrylic finish, seal the pumpkin to prolong the life of the carving.

40

This is the finished carving.

PART THREE

EXTREME PUMPKIN PATTERNS

Each pattern in this book is drawn to an appropriate size for most pumpkins. To use a pattern, first photocopy or trace the pattern of your choice. Compare the size and shape of the pumpkin with the size and shape of the pattern. Enlarge or reduce the pattern to fit the pumpkin.

Next tape the pattern to the pumpkin in preparation for transferring. Because of the curvature of the pumpkin, most patterns will wrinkle. To prevent this, cut the paper at the wrinkles and re-tape it. You will experience a little distortion but not enough to significantly alter the pattern.

Finally transfer the pattern to the pumpkin with a nail or a pounce wheel. Be sure to outline all of the main features of the pumpkin, such as face shape, eyes, nose, mouth, teeth, hair and so on. The shaded areas of the pattern indicate depth of cut and do not need to be transferred. As you carve, you will want to refer to the pattern frequently to gauge how deeply to cut. Lightly shaded areas are very shallow; heavily shaded areas are deeply carved.

By Gary Falin

By Mike Jenkins

By Renee Manning

By Renee Manning

By Tony Harris

By Vic Hood

By Wayne Shinlever

PART THREE

PART THREE

More Great Books from Fox Chapel Publishing

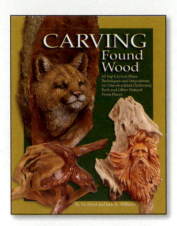

Carving Found Wood
ISBN 978-1-56523-159-7 **$19.95**

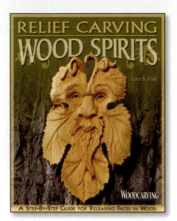

Relief Carving Wood Spirits
ISBN 978-1-56523-333-1 **$19.95**

Homemade Halloween
ISBN 978-1-56523-382-9 **$14.95**

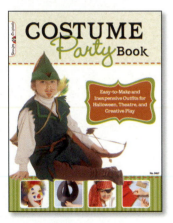

Costume Party Book
ISBN 978-1-57421-344-7 **$9.99**

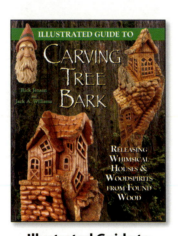

**Illustrated Guide to
Carving Tree Bark**
ISBN 978-1-56523-218-1 **$14.95**

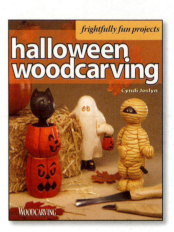

Halloween Woodcarving
ISBN 978-1-56523-289-1 **$16.95**

In addition to being a leading source of woodworking books and DVDs, Fox Chapel also publishes two premiere magazines. Released quarterly, each delivers premium projects, expert tips and techniques from today's finest woodworking artists, and in-depth information about the latest tools, equipment, and materials.

Subscribe Today!
Woodcarving Illustrated: **888-506-6630**
Scroll Saw Woodworking & Crafts: **888-840-8590**
www.FoxChapelPublishing.com